Canadian Curriculum

ScienceSmart

Grade 2

ISBN: 978-1-927042-84-7

Copyright © 2013 Popular Book Company (Canada) Limited

Printed in China

Contents

ISBN: 978-1-927042-84-7

ISBN: 978-1-927042-84-7

ISBN: 978-1-927042-84-7

Growth and Changes in Living Things

As we grow, our bodies go through lots of changes. Some animals change greatly, others not so much, just like how your baby sister will grow up like you.

In this unit, students will:

- compare the appearance of young and mature animals of the same species and know their names.
- understand the life cycles of living things.
- identify the characteristics that animals have in their adulthood.

ISBN: 978-1-927042-84-7

1

A. **Write the names of the baby animals. Then draw lines to match the babies with what they will grow up to be.**

calf   chick   cub   fawn   piglet

_____ •

_____ •

_____ •

• hen
• cow
• pig
• bear
• deer

_____ •

_____ •

Science Corner ....

A newborn kangaroo (joey) is about the length of your thumb, while some baby giraffes (calves) are as tall as a door when they are born.

ISBN: 978-1-927042-84-7

B. Number the pictures to show the order of growth.

1.

2.

3.

ISBN: 978-1-927042-84-7

1

C. **Fill in the blanks. Then write 1 to 4 to show the life cycle of a Monarch butterfly.**

Life Cycle of a Monarch Butterfly

caterpillar   butterfly
egg   chrysalis

A Monarch butterfly lays her

1. _____ on a leaf. The

egg hatches in about five days

and becomes a 2._____ .

The caterpillar then attaches

itself to a twig and becomes

a 3._____ . After about

two weeks, the 4._____

emerges from the chrysalis.

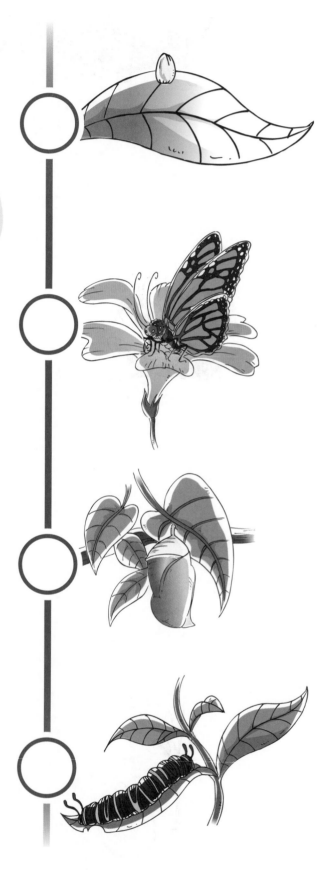

D. Name the animal classes. Then match the descriptions with the correct classes.

mammals
birds
insects
reptiles

Ⓐ They have two antennae and six legs.

Ⓑ Mothers give birth to live young.

Ⓒ They are covered in scales.

Ⓓ They have feathers.

1.

2.

3.

4.

1

How Much Have You Grown?

Ask your friends how tall they were when they were born. Then measure their current heights. Record them in a chart and find the differences. Find who has grown the most.

Name	Height at Birth	Current Height	Difference

Checklist

Are you able to...

☐ relate the young and mature animals of the same species and tell their names?

☐ describe the life cycles of living things?

☐ identify the characteristics that animals have in their adulthood?

ISBN: 978-1-927042-84-7

Animal Adaptation

2

I want to store up food like you to get ready for winter.

No, you don't have to because you'll go into hibernation, which means you'll sleep through the winter.

In this unit, students will:

- identify the characteristics of some animals.
- identify predators and prey and tell how their characteristics benefit them in their roles.
- understand the behavioural characteristics that enable animals to survive.

ISBN: 978-1-927042-84-7

2

A. **Put the letters in the correct circles to show the characteristics of each animal.**

Animals that have:

A fur

B feathers

C wings

D scales

E moist, smooth skin

F no legs

G 4 legs

1.

2.

3.

4.

5.

ISBN: 978-1-927042-84-7

B. **Do the matching. Write "predator" or "prey" in the boxes. Then match the animals with their characteristics that benefit them in their roles.**

predator •   • an animal that gets hunted for food

prey •   • an animal that hunts another animal for food

Scenario 1

lynx

snowshoe hare

• It is a fast runner.

• It is as white as snow.

Scenario 2

fly

frog

• It has a sticky tongue.

• It flies very fast.

ISBN: 978-1-927042-84-7

2

C. Fill in the blanks to complete the passage.

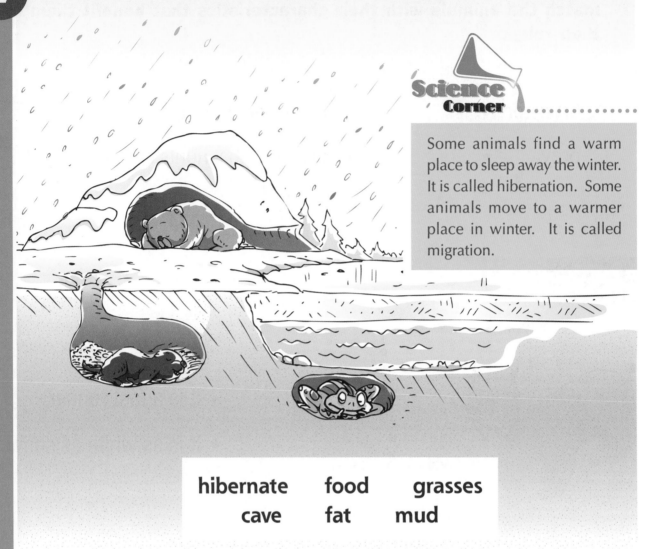

Science Corner ....

Some animals find a warm place to sleep away the winter. It is called hibernation. Some animals move to a warmer place in winter. It is called migration.

hibernate   food   grasses
cave   fat   mud

It is getting cold. Groundhog has eaten many seeds and

1._____ . *He goes into his underground burrow to*

2._____ *for the winter. Bear is also getting ready for a*

long winter in her den or 3._____ . *Near the pond, Frog*

has buried himself in 4._____ . *Like Groundhog, Bear,*

and many other animals, his body will slow down enough that

he will have little need for 5._____ . *He can live off his*

extra stored 6._____ .

D. Write the correct ending for each of these migration verses.

1. I migrate in water

   for I am a whale.

   Swimming south in the winter

   _____ .

- I pick up the mail
- I buy a new tail
- I return without fail

2. We're Monarch butterflies.

   We gather, then go.

   We don't want to stay for

   _____ .

- the flower show
- the wind and the snow
- Peter or Joe

3. Some birds in the winter

   are not to be found.

   They've migrated south to

   _____ .

- twirl round and round
- a good feeding ground
- make a loud sound

ISBN: 978-1-927042-84-7

2

Animal Camouflage

To stay safe from predators, many animals adopt camouflage, that is, they blend themselves into their surroundings so that they cannot be spotted easily. Do this experiment to see how camouflage works.

Steps:

1. Draw and colour the animals on sheets of paper.

2. Cut the animals out and place them on a piece of green construction paper.

3. Ask a friend to name all the animals. Which animal did your friend name first? Which one was named last? Do you know why?

Are you able to...

- ☐ identify the characteristics of some animals?
- ☐ identify predators and prey and tell how their characteristics benefit them in their roles?
- ☐ describe the behavioural characteristics that enable animals to survive?

ISBN: 978-1-927042-84-7

Human and Animal Interactions

3

I think bees are great because they make honey for us.

Yes, they are good. But they're going to sting us!

In this unit, students will:

- learn how some animals benefit or harm us.
- understand that some human activities can harm animals.
- identify ways to protect animals.

ISBN: 978-1-927042-84-7

3

A. Read the descriptions to see how some animals benefit us. Then write the names of the animals being described.

How Animals **Benefit Us**

dogs   sheep

bats   bees   birds

1. They provide us with honey.

_____

2. They help control the mosquito population.

_____

3. They provide pleasurable viewing experiences across the sky.

_____

4 They provide us with wool for warm clothing.

_____

5 They may be trained to be the eyes for people who cannot see.

_____

ISBN: 978-1-927042-84-7

B. Fill in the blanks and circle the correct words to see how animals harm us.

birds   mosquitoes
moose   bee

1.

_____ spread diseases / pollens through their bites.

2.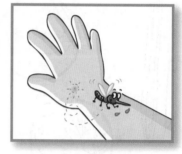

_____ , deer, and bears on roads pose hazards to drivers / plants .

3.

_____ destroy meat / crops such as apples and blackberries.

4.

Some people are allergic to wasp and _____ venoms / wings from their stingers.

ISBN: 978-1-927042-84-7

3

C. Read how human activities harm animals. Then colour the animals that are affected by each human activity.

Human Activities that Harm Animals

1.

NEWS

Humans use pesticides to kill insects in their lawns.

2.

NEWS

Humans kill animals for their skins and furs to use for clothing.

STOP!

3.

NEWS

Humans hunt wild animals for sport.

ISBN: 978-1-927042-84-7

D. Circle the correct words to find out how we can protect animals.

How We Can Protect Animals

To protect endangered animals:

protected   homes   hunting

preventing pollution and land development to protect animals' 1._____

building 2._____ parks and reserves for animals and their babies

banning people from 3._____ animals

To protect unwanted pets:

adopt   food   shelter

providing pets with basic needs such as 4._____ and 5._____

encouraging people to 6._____ pets rather than buy new ones

ISBN: 978-1-927042-84-7

3

Animals Around Us

Animals are all around us: squirrels in trees, worms in soil, and even spiders in our houses! Observe and check ✔ the animals that you have seen in five days.

Animals I Have Seen in 5 Days

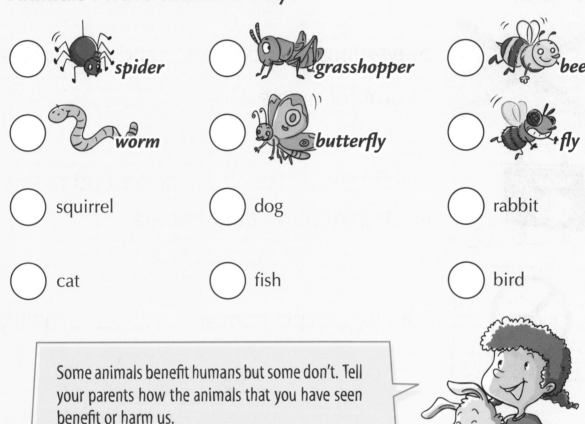

- ◯ *spider*
- ◯ *grasshopper*
- ◯ *bee*
- ◯ *worm*
- ◯ *butterfly*
- ◯ *fly*
- ◯ squirrel
- ◯ dog
- ◯ rabbit
- ◯ cat
- ◯ fish
- ◯ bird

Some animals benefit humans but some don't. Tell your parents how the animals that you have seen benefit or harm us.

Checklist

Are you able to...

- ☐ explain how some animals benefit or harm us?
- ☐ describe some human activities that harm animals?
- ☐ identify ways to protect animals?

Three States of Water

In this unit, students will:

- identify the three states of water.
- understand how water changes its state.
- identify whether heat is added or taken away in each change of state.

4

A. Water comes in 3 forms. Read what Mike says and unscramble the letters to reveal the different states of water. Then write the states of water shown in the pictures.

It must be cold. **(dosli)**

1. _____

Science Corner

All the water there has ever been on Earth (as a gas, liquid, or solid) is all the water that is on Earth now.

You drink it. **(iilqud)**

2. _____

It's invisible. **(sag)**

3. _____

4. _____

5. _____

6. _____

7. _____

ISBN: 978-1-927042-84-7

B. Fill in the blanks to complete the passage. Then draw the correct pictures to show how water changes its state.

freeze   melt   evaporate

The same water that makes up an ice cube may

1._____ in the water you drink. When

heated, that same water may 2._____ into

gas (called vapour) in the air you breathe. And it

may 3._____ and become an ice cube again.

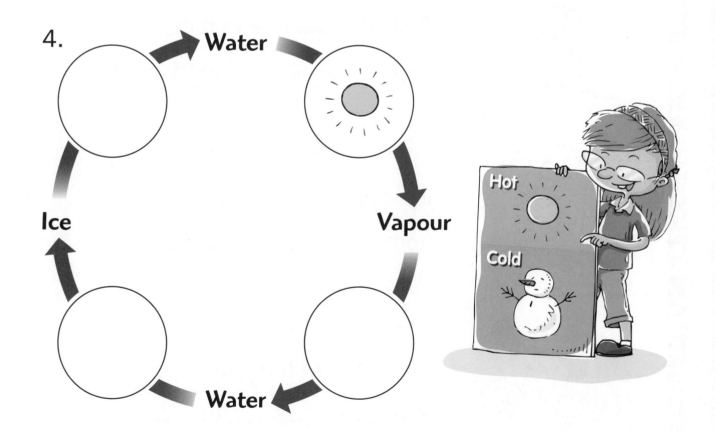

4

C. Look at the change in the state of water in each picture. Fill in the blanks.

1.

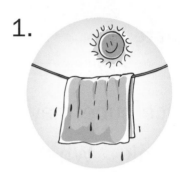

Wet towel hung to dry:

from _____ to _____

2.

Water on a skating rink:

from _____ to _____

3.

Boiling water in a kettle:

from _____ to _____

4.

Ice cubes in a glass:

from _____ to _____

5.

Snowman in the sun:

from _____ to _____

ISBN: 978-1-927042-84-7

D. Write each state of water. Colour the correct picture to show where the change takes place.

1.

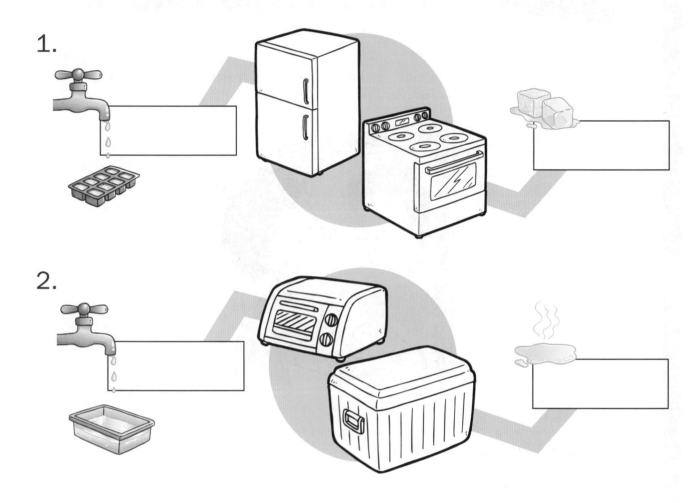

2.

E. Write "cooling" or "heating".

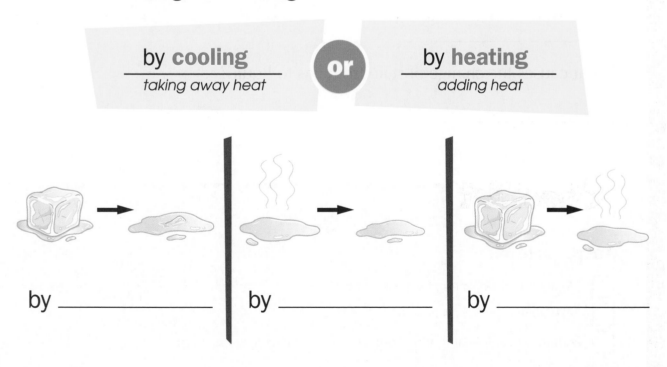

4

From Gas to Liquid!

See how gas changes to liquid. Exhale close to a mirror or a window.

Can you see the water on the mirror?

_____

Where does the water come from?

_____

What causes the change of state from gas to liquid?

_____

Are you able to...

- [ ] identify the three states of water?
- [ ] tell how water changes its state?
- [ ] identify whether heat is added or taken away in each change of state?

ISBN: 978-1-927042-84-7

Liquids and Solids (1)

In this unit, students will:

- understand the properties of liquids and solids.
- recognize the states of liquids and solids in different circumstances.
- understand the meaning of buoyancy.
- identify situations where liquids are repelled and where they are absorbed.

ISBN: 978-1-927042-84-7

5

A. Write "liquid" or "solid" to tell what each verse is about. Then sort the things into the correct groups. Write the letters in the circles.

1. It has a shape

   It has a size

   Not easy to change

   Before your eyes

   It is a _____ .

2. It flows, it pours

   It's thick, it's thin

   It takes the shape

   Of whatever it's in

   It is a _____ .

ISBN: 978-1-927042-84-7

B. Tell the states of the things. Then check ✔ the correct sentences to describe the pictures.

1.

Before   ⟶   After

_____   _____

(A) Ice melts when heated.

(B) Ice freezes when heated.

2. Before   After

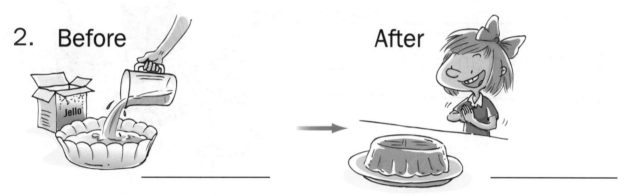

_____   _____

(A) Jello melts when chilled.

(B) Jello becomes solid when chilled.

3. Before   After

_____   _____

(A) Solids remain solid when broken.

(B) Solids change to liquid when broken.

ISBN: 978-1-927042-84-7

5

C. Fill in the blanks. Then colour the objects that are buoyant.

Buoyancy

buoyant   water   float

Buoyancy is the ability of something to 1._____ on a liquid. For example, beach balls are 2._____ because they can float on 3._____ .

4.

ISBN: 978-1-927042-84-7

D. Do the matching to describe the items.

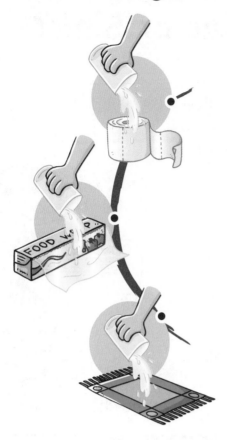

- It **repels** liquids.

- It **absorbs** liquids.

E. What happens to the liquids? Write the letters in the correct circles.

1.

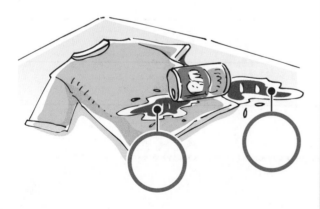

A It will be absorbed.

B It can be wiped up by a towel.

2.

A It will be repelled.

B It will be absorbed.

ISBN: 978-1-927042-84-7

5

Does It Float or Sink?

Some things float and some don't. Do this activity to see whether the things float or sink.

Don't forget to have your parents' approval before you do this activity.

Steps:

1. Fill up a bucket or sink with water.

2. Choose some objects that are small enough to be placed in the water.

3. Guess whether each object will float or sink when placed in the water.

4. Put the objects in the water. Record your results in the chart.

Object	My guess	My observation

Checklist

Are you able to...

- [ ] tell the properties of liquids and solids?
- [ ] recognize the states of liquids and solids in different circumstances?
- [ ] tell the meaning of buoyancy?
- [ ] identify situations where liquids are repelled and where they are absorbed?

ISBN: 978-1-927042-84-7

A. Complete the crossword puzzle.

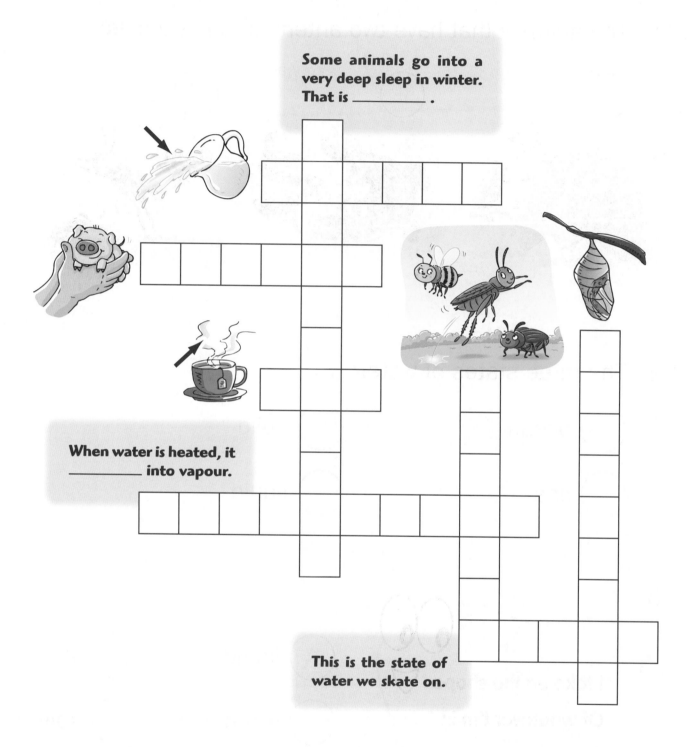

Some animals go into a very deep sleep in winter. That is _____ .

When water is heated, it _____ into vapour.

This is the state of water we skate on.

piglet chrysalis insects liquid

gas evaporates solid hibernation

ISBN: 978-1-927042-84-7

B.   Check ✔ the correct answers.

1. The animals that have two antennae and six legs:

2. The three states of water:

(A) ocean

(B) solid

(C) gas

(D) liquid

3.

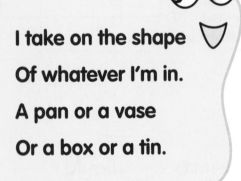

I take on the shape

Of whatever I'm in.

A pan or a vase

Or a box or a tin.

(A) liquid

(B) sun

(C) winter

(D) solid

ISBN: 978-1-927042-84-7

4. The sentence that describes the picture:

   (A) Ice melts when heated.

   (B) Water evaporates when heated.

   (C) Water freezes when cooled.

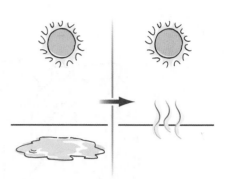

5. The buoyant objects:

6. The one that shows a dragonfly's order of growth:

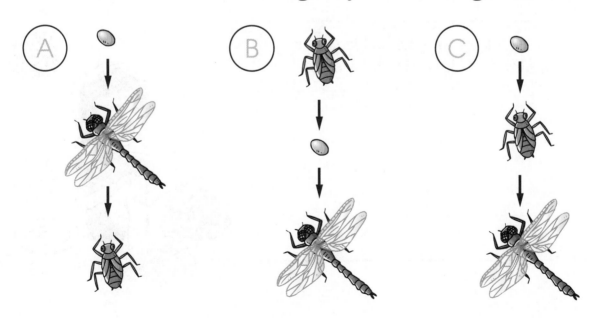

C. Here are some items used in cooking. List them beside the mixing bowl if they are solid, and beside the measuring cup if they are liquid.

D. Answer the question.

> If I leave a dish of water in the open in good weather, what will happen after a few days?

Liquids and Solids (2)

6

You shouldn't touch these things, Tiffany. They are dangerous.

flammable   explosive

poisonous   corrosive

In this unit, students will:

- identify the properties of some liquids and solids.
- distinguish between solids that dissolve in water and solids that do not.
- identify solutions that are formed by mixing solids with liquids.
- recognize hazard symbols and their meanings.

6

A. Match each object with its properties.

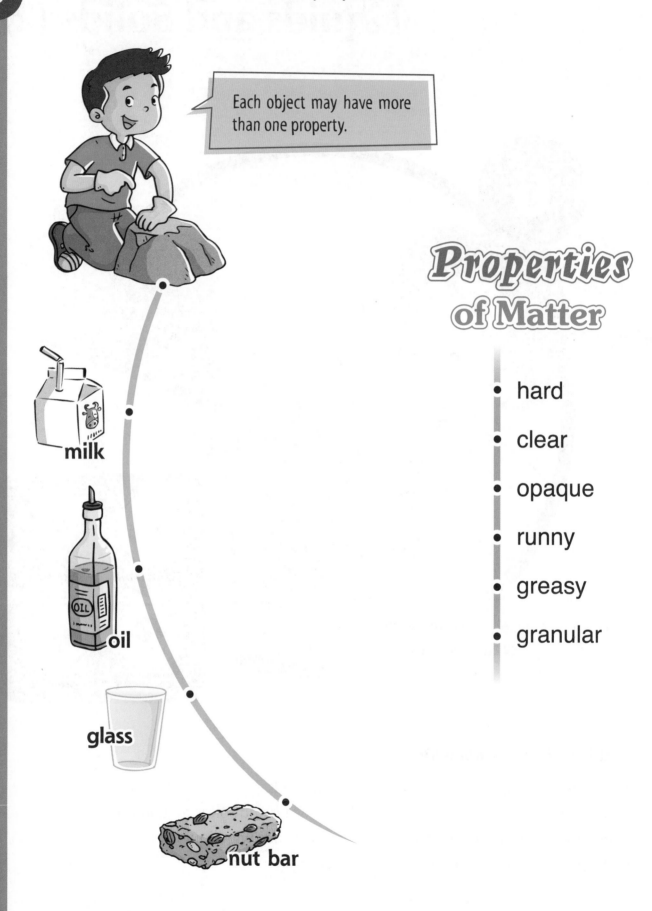

Each object may have more than one property.

milk

oil

glass

nut bar

Properties of Matter

- hard
- clear
- opaque
- runny
- greasy
- granular

ISBN: 978-1-927042-84-7

B. Mix a spoonful of each solid in a cup of warm water. Record which of these solids dissolve in water. Check ✔ the correct boxes. Then answer the questions.

warm water

Science Corner

What happens when a solid is mixed with a liquid? Some solids stay solid, but some solids dissolve. The solid is no longer a solid. Together with the liquid, it forms a solution.

1.

Solid	Sugar	Salt	Rice	Sand
Dissolves				
Does not dissolve				

2. What happened to the solids that dissolved?

_____

3. What happened to the solids that did not dissolve?

_____

4.

What do we call the liquid after sugar is added to water?

_____

6

C. **Does each pair of solid and liquid form a solution? Draw a line to "Solution" if it does.**

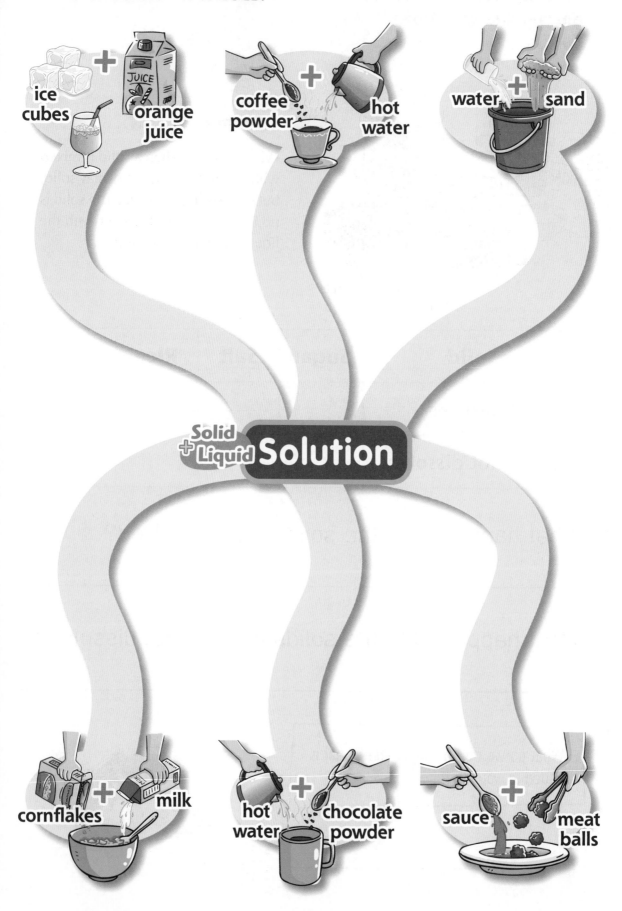

ISBN: 978-1-927042-84-7

D. Trace the frames and fill in the blanks to complete the names of the hazard symbols. Then match the symbols with the correct warning messages. Write the letters.

corrosive	explosive	flammable	poisonous

1.

___o___ ___osiv___ ◯

2.

___la___ ___abl___ ◯

3.

___oi___ ___nous ◯

4.

___ ___plosi___ ___ ◯

A This could catch fire easily.

B This could burn your skin or eyes.

C If heated or punctured, this could explode.

D If you swallow or inhale this, you could get sick or die.

Science Corner ....

There are two frames for the symbols.

▽ : means that the container is dangerous

◯ : means that the contents inside the container are dangerous

6

 **Try this**

Mixing Liquids

Does mixing two liquids make a solution?
Try this experiment to find out.

> Fill the cups to about one-third full.

Materials:
- cooking oil
- white vinegar
- 2 clear cups

Steps:

1. Add some water to both cups.

2. Pour some oil into one cup and some vinegar into the other.

3. Observe the liquids.

Do both liquids form a solution with water?   Yes / No

Which liquid forms a solution with water?   oil / vinegar

 **Checklist**

Are you able to...

- [ ] identify the properties of some liquids and solids?
- [ ] distinguish between solids that dissolve in water and solids that do not?
- [ ] identify solutions that are formed by mixing solids with liquids?
- [ ] recognize hazard symbols and their meanings?

ISBN: 978-1-927042-84-7

Movements and Positions

In this unit, students will:

- describe the positions and movements of objects.
- describe the patterns of movement of objects.

7

A. Look at the picture. Describe where the things are by using the given position words.

beside	behind	under	over	in front of

1. The girl is standing _____ the rack of toys.

2. The fly is flying _____ the soldier.

3. The rabbit is _____ the snake.

4. The cow is _____ the robot.

5. The cat is _____ the robot.

B. Circle the better words to complete the sentences.

1. Pour the sand   under / into   the pail.

2. The children crawled   in / under   the slide and went

   beside / through   the tunnel.

ISBN: 978-1-927042-84-7

C. **Jason has to move left, right, up, or down by squares to get to his toys. Help him draw the pictures and describe the movements.**

1. The animal Jason gets to if he goes:

    a. 2 left and 1 up

    b. 1 right and 2 down

2. Jason gets to the octopus: _____

3. Jason gets to the cow: _____

4. If Jason goes 1 left and 2 down, he gets to . Draw  in the grid.

ISBN: 978-1-927042-84-7

7

D. Trace the dotted lines and describe the movements with the given words.

> back and forth   round and round
>
> up and down   straight

1.

_____

2.

_____

3.

_____

4.

_____

Canadian Curriculum ScienceSmart • **Grade 2**   ISBN: 978-1-927042-84-7

E. Choose the correct words to describe the patterns of movement.

spinning	swinging	turning
bouncing	rolling	sliding

Science Corner

Movement happens everywhere. We create it all the time. We use special words to describe different kinds of movement.

1.

A _____

B _____

C _____

2. _____

3. _____

4. _____

7

A Rolling Marble

Through this experiment you see how the movements of a marble can be affected by different surfaces.

Materials:

- books
- a marble
- surfaces to compare the marble's movements: floor, carpet, grass, sandpaper, etc.

Steps:

1. Make a ramp using the books.

2. Roll the marble down the ramp onto the various surfaces.

3. Record your observations.

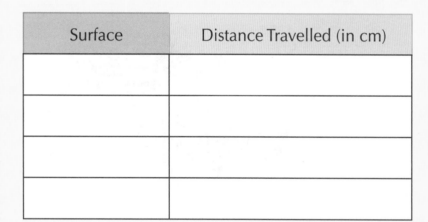

Surface	Distance Travelled (in cm)

Can you see that the distances the marble travelled are different on different surfaces?

Are you able to...

☐ describe the positions and movements of objects?

☐ describe the patterns of movement of objects?

ISBN: 978-1-927042-84-7

Simple Machines

8

inclined plane

We can use simple machines to make work easier.

lever

In this unit, students will:

- identify different kinds of simple machines.
- understand how simple machines enable objects to move.
- understand how two simple machines can be put together to form a new machine.

8

A. **Read the description of each kind of simple machine. Colour the two pictures that are examples of each simple machine.**

1. **Wheel and Axle**

It is a wheel attached to an axle.

2. **Pulley**

It is a wheel with a string or rope wrapped around it.

3. **Lever**

It makes lifting, cutting, or moving something easier.

 Canadian Curriculum ScienceSmart • **Grade 2**   ISBN: 978-1-927042-84-7

4. Inclined Plane

It is always on a slant. It helps lift a load or get it down.

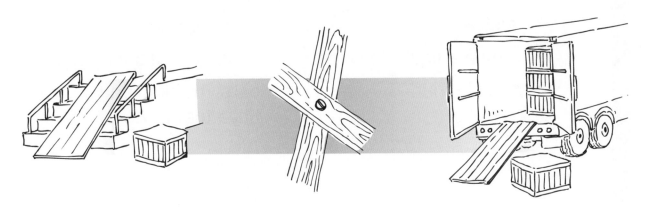

5. Screw

It is like an inclined plane that is wrapped around something.

Home
Sweet
Home

6. Wedge

It is a back-to-back inclined plane. It may hold things together or pull things apart.

ISBN: 978-1-927042-84-7

8

B. **Read the clues. Guess what machines the children are describing. Write the answers.**

- crack a nut
- turn on a light
- lift a big man

1. _____

- turn together
- make pulling things easier
- cars, trucks, and buses have them

2. _____

- pull rope down, object goes up
- found on a clothesline or a flagpole
- looks like a wheel

3. _____

- flat, leaning surface
- helps move things onto a higher platform
- does not look like a tool

4. _____

- lowers or raises things
- holds things together

5. _____

- pencil sharpener, knife, nail, etc.
- back-to-back inclined plane, making a sharp edge

6. _____

ISBN: 978-1-927042-84-7

C. **See which two simple machines are put together to form a new machine. Read the rhyme and colour the described machine. Then label its parts.**

1. *Wedge and Lever*
   See what I'll do
   I can snip and cut
   Trim the bangs of Mindy Lou

2. *Lever, Wheel and Axle*
   I lift the things you want to see gone
   And roll them all around the place
   'Til you tell me to dump them down

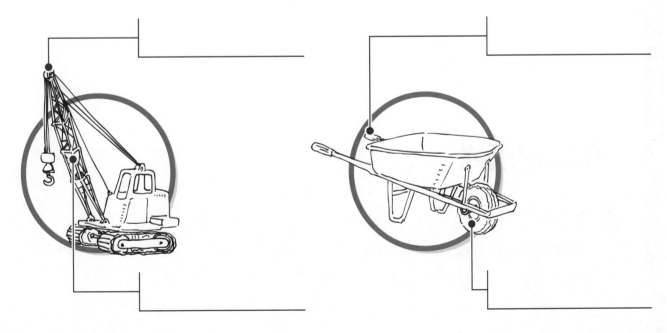

ISBN: 978-1-927042-84-7

8

A Model of a Simple Machine

You can make a model of a simple machine.

Materials:

- a slope-shaped piece of paper
- a pencil
- tape

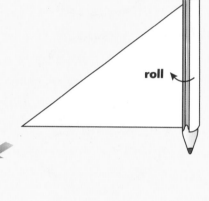

roll

> Wind the paper around the pencil and tape it. Do you know what you've made?

Checklist

Are you able to...

☐ identify different kinds of simple machines?

☐ tell how simple machines enable objects to move?

☐ show how two simple machines can be put together to form a new machine?

Air in the Environment

In this unit, students will:

- use different things to show evidence of air.
- understand the meaning of temperature.
- understand the causes of air pollution.

ISBN: 978-1-927042-84-7

9

A. Fill in the blanks to show the uses of air.

plants	sailboat	seeds
windmill	hot-air balloons	

1.

Air disperses _____ .

2.

Air keeps a _____ moving.

3. Air keeps _____ flying in the sky.

4. Air turns a _____ to make electricity.

5. Animals and _____ need air to live and grow.

ISBN: 978-1-927042-84-7

B. Match the pictures with the descriptions. Write the letters.

A

B

C

D

E

F

Air takes up space.

Examples: Air fills up the balloon.

Air makes things move.

Examples:

Moving air (wind) makes the pinwheel turn.

9

C. **Fill in the blanks with the given words. Then check ✔ the correct answers.**

The 1._____ of air shows how hot or cold the air is. We measure temperature with a 2._____ . The unit of measure is 3._____ (˚C).

degree Celsius

temperature

thermometer

4.

What tool do I use to measure temperature?

(A) a thermometer (B) a measuring cup

(C) a scale (D) a ruler

5.

What temperature is this thermometer showing?

(A) 15˚C (B) 20˚C

(C) 25˚C (D) 30˚C

6.

Which season is it?

(A) spring (B) summer

(C) fall (D) winter

D. Read the passage. Then answer the questions.

Harmful gases and particles in the air cause pollution. Burning your trash pollutes the air. Driving a car pollutes the air. Smoke from factories pollutes the air.

Polluted air travels from one place to other places by wind.

Sometimes polluted air mixes with water vapour. This makes acid rain. When acid rain falls, it can damage plants and other things.

1. What are three things that cause air pollution?

   _____

   _____

   _____

2. How does polluted air travel?

   _____

   _____

3. What causes acid rain?

   _____

   _____

9

Make a Fan!

Make a fan with a piece of paper and try it in different places in your house and outside. You can find that air is around us.

Steps:

1.

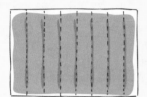

Fold along the dotted lines.

Materials:

- a piece of paper
- glue

2.

Fold it up and glue the ends.

glue

Fan yourself with it. Do you feel a breeze? That's moving air, or wind.

3.

Open it.

Checklist

Are you able to...

- [ ] use different things to show evidence of air?
- [ ] tell what temperature is?
- [ ] point out the causes of air pollution?

Canadian Curriculum ScienceSmart • **Grade 2**
ISBN: 978-1-927042-84-7

Water in the Environment

In this unit, students will:

- learn how water changes in nature.
- identify the different forms of moisture in the air.
- find out where we get water and how water gets to us.
- learn ways to save water.

ISBN: 978-1-927042-84-7

10

A. **Match each event happening in the picture with the correct description. Write the letter.**

Most water that falls to the ground seeps underground. It may end up in the ocean.

1. ◯
   Water vapour condenses in the air. I can see it now.

2. Water is evaporating into the air. ◯

3. Plants and animals take in water and release it as vapour or liquid. ◯

4. It was vapour, but it got frozen and is falling to the ground. ◯

5. Vapour is returning to Earth in the form of liquid. ◯

ISBN: 978-1-927042-84-7

B. **Which form of moisture is the answer to each riddle? Solve the riddle and write the answer.**

dew   hail   snow   rain   fog   frost

1.

   It is a cloud close to the ground.

   _____

2. They are solid, and no two of these crystals are exactly alike.

   _____

3. They are bits of ice from the sky.

   _____

4. It happens in the morning. It did not rain, yet everything is wet.

   _____

5. You may see this in a winter morning. Water vapour has turned to ice crystals.

   _____

6. It is liquid. It falls from dark clouds in the sky.

   _____

10

C. **Unscramble the letters. Then label the diagram with the words in bold.**

Where do we get water?

e l **w** l

1. _____

v r i e **r**

2. _____

a l **e** k

3. _____

How does lake water get to us?

*In some cities, water is moved from a lake to a human-made **water treatment plant** where it is cleaned so that it is safe to drink. It is then distributed to homes through a **water supply system** of pipes and pumps.*

4. _____

It takes a lot of effort to get clean water, so never waste water.

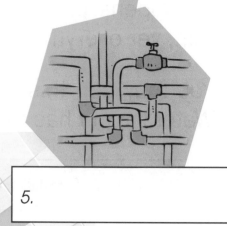

5. _____

ISBN: 978-1-927042-84-7

D. **Match the pictures with the descriptions to see how we can save water. Then make a suggestion.**

Ways to Save Water:

☐ Turn off the faucet while brushing your teeth.

☐ Take a shower instead of a bath.

☐ Run a dishwasher only when it is a full load.

☐ Fix leaky faucets.

My suggestion: _____

_____

10

Make Rain!

Follow the steps below to make "rain".
Ask an adult to help you.

Materials:

- 2 dishes
- an electric kettle

Steps:

1. Boil some water in the electric kettle.

2. When the water boils, place a dish over the mouth of the kettle to catch the water vapour.

3. Catch the "rain" with the other dish.

It's raining!

In nature, water vapour condenses and becomes clouds. Check ✔ the one that represents vapour.

A   B   C

Checklist

Are you able to...

- [ ] describe how water changes in nature?
- [ ] identify the different forms of moisture in the air?
- [ ] tell where we get water and how water gets to us?
- [ ] tell ways to save water?

A. Complete the crossword puzzle.

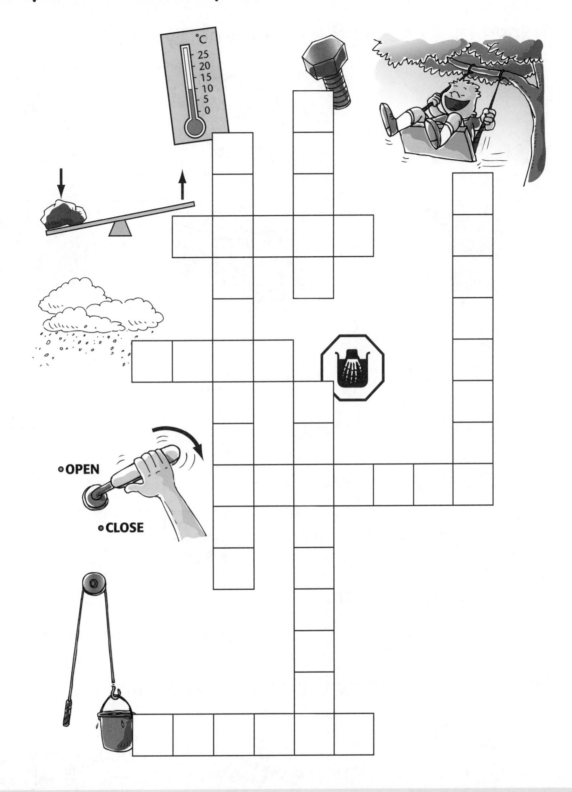

thermometer   lever   pulley   screw

corrosive   swinging   snow   turning

B. Check ✔ the correct answers.

1. Things that use wind as their energy source:

2. Move the rabbit to the cat:

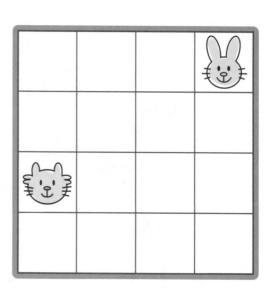

A) 3 right and 2 down

B) 3 left and 2 down

C) 2 right and 3 down

D) 2 right and 3 up

3. The items that show the existence of air:

ISBN: 978-1-927042-84-7

4. Examples of levers:

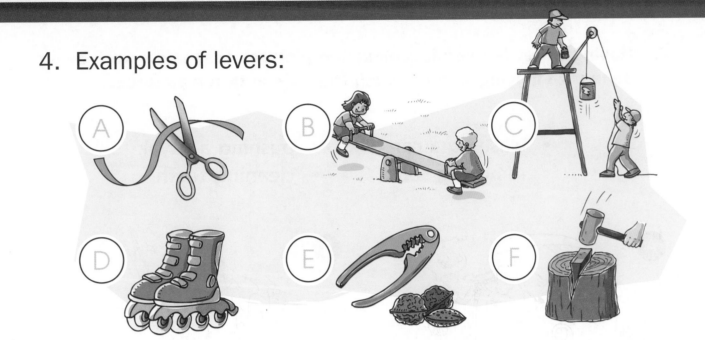

5. The animals that have scales and no legs:

A) fish

B) bird

C) frog

D) snake

6. Sources of water:

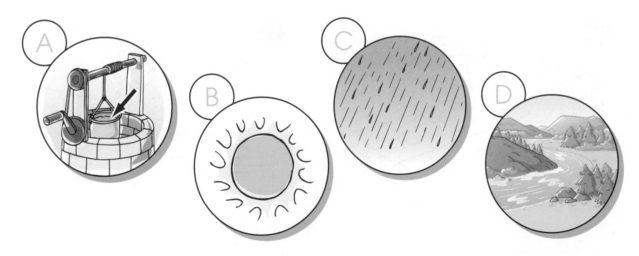

ISBN: 978-1-927042-84-7

C. **Moving water is useful. Colour the pictures that show work being done with moving water. Match the uses with the pictures.**

- washing a car
- removing suds
- pushing a kayak
- cleaning teeth

A

_____

B

_____

C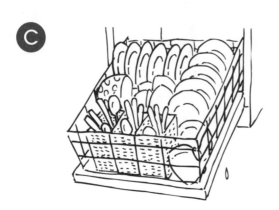

_____

D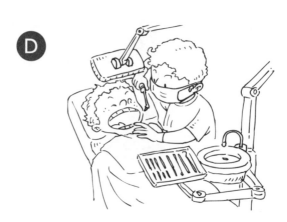

_____

E

_____

F

_____

ISBN: 978-1-927042-84-7

D. Read what the children say. Help them find the correct tools. Write the letters.

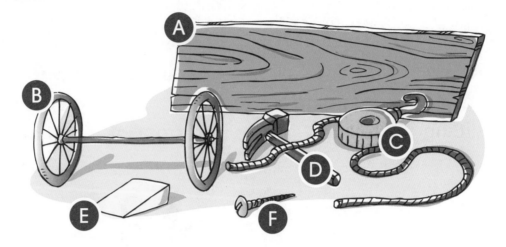

1.  I want to remove the nails on the door. ◯

2. I want to fasten the door. ◯

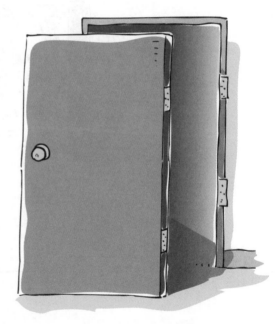

3.

I want to move this wooden box to a different spot on this floor. ◯

I want to move this wooden box to a place accessed by stairs. ◯

ISBN: 978-1-927042-84-7

E. **Look at this picture. Choose the correct movement words and position words to complete the sentences.**

pulling	turning	under	over
bouncing	swinging	in	on
sliding	rolling	in front of	behind

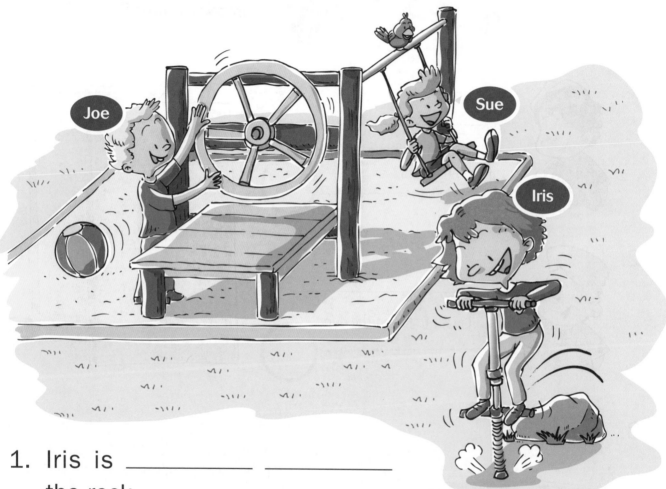

1. Iris is _____ _____ the rock.

2. Joe is _____ the wheel _____ the playground set.

3. Sue is _____ _____ the bird.

4. The ball is _____ _____ Joe.

ISBN: 978-1-927042-84-7

Answers

ANSWERS

1 Growth and Changes in Living Things

A.

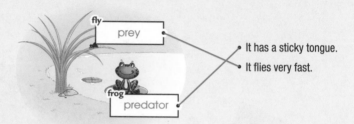

chick — hen
cub — bear
piglet — pig
calf — cow
fawn — deer

B. 1. 3 ; 2 ; 1
2. 4 ; 1 ; 3 ; 2
3. 2 ; 1 ; 4 ; 3
C. 1. egg   2. caterpillar
3. chrysalis   4. butterfly
1 ; 4 ; 3 ; 2
D. 1. insects ; A
2. reptiles ; C
3. birds ; D
4. mammals ; B

Try this!
Activity

2 Animal Adaptations

A. 1. D ; F
2. E ; G
3. D ; F
4. B ; C
5. A ; G
B. predator — an animal that gets hunted for food
prey — an animal that hunts another animal for food

Scenario 1:

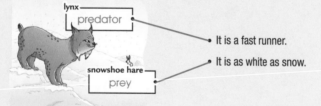

lynx — predator — It is a fast runner.
snowshoe hare — prey — It is as white as snow.

Scenario 2:

fly — prey — It has a sticky tongue.
frog — predator — It flies very fast.

C. 1. grasses
2. hibernate
3. cave
4. mud
5. food
6. fat
D. 1. I return without fail
2. the wind and the snow
3. a good feeding ground

Try this!
Activity

3 Human and Animal Interactions

A. 1. bees
2. bats
3. birds
4. sheep
5. dogs
B. 1. Mosquitoes ; diseases
2. Moose ; drivers
3. Birds ; crops
4. bee ; venoms
C. 1.

2.

3.

ISBN: 978-1-927042-84-7

D. 1. homes
    2. protected
    3. hunting
    4. food
    5. shelter
    6. adopt

Try this!
    Activity

4 Three States of Water

A. 1. solid
    2. liquid
    3. gas
    4. gas
    5. liquid
    6. solid
    7. gas
B. 1. melt
    2. evaporate
    3. freeze
    4.

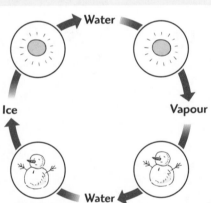

C. 1. liquid ; gas
    2. liquid ; solid
    3. liquid ; gas
    4. solid ; liquid
    5. solid ; liquid
D. 1. liquid ; ; solid

    2. liquid ; ; gas

E. heating ; cooling ; heating

Try this!
    yes
    the air
    the warm air

5 Liquids and Solids (1)

A. 1. solid ; A ; D ; F
    2. liquid ; B ; C ; E
B. 1. solid ; liquid ; Ice melts when heated.
    2. liquid ; solid ; Jello becomes solid when chilled.
    3. solid ; solid ; Solids remain solid when broken.
C. 1. float
    2. buoyant
    3. water
    4.

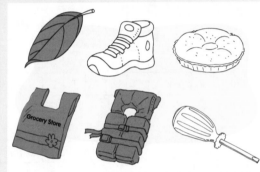

D.

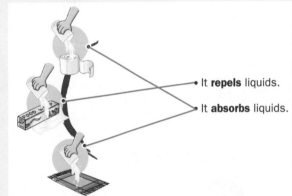

It **repels** liquids.
It **absorbs** liquids.

E. 1.

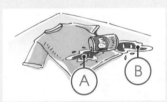

    2.

Try this!
    Activity

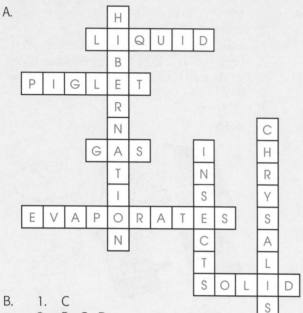

Midway Review

A.

```
        H
   [L] I Q U I D
        I
 P I G[L]E T
        R
        N
        A
     G A S      I        C
        T        N       H
        I        S       R
                 E       Y
 E V A P O R A T E S     S
        N        C       A
                 T       L
               [S]O L I D
                         I
                         S
```

B.
1. C
2. B ; C ; D
3. A
4. B
5. C ; D ; F
6. C

C. Solid: flour ; almonds ; chocolate chips ; cheese
   Liquid: milk ; vegetable oil ; honey ; juice

D. The water in the dish will evaporate.

6 Liquids and Solids (2)

A.
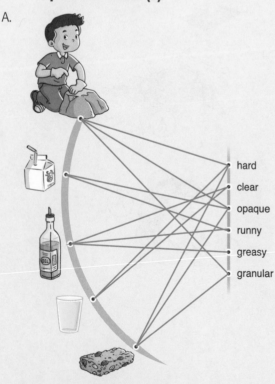

hard
clear
opaque
runny
greasy
granular

B.
1. Dissolves: Sugar ; Salt
   Does not dissolve: Rice ; Sand
2. The solids could not be seen anymore.
3. The solids could still be seen in the water.
4. solution

C.
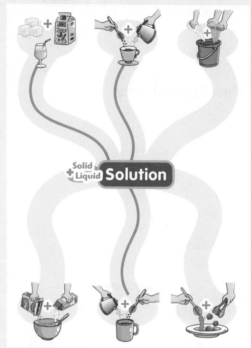

D. Trace the frames.
1. corrosive ; B   2. flammable ; A
3. poisonous ; D   4. explosive ; C

Try this!
   No
   vinegar

7 Movements and Positions

A.
1. behind   2. over
3. beside   4. under
5. in front of

B.
1. into   2. under ; through

C. 1a.   b.

2. 3 right
3. 2 left and 1 down
4.

ISBN: 978-1-927042-84-7

D. Trace the dotted lines.
1. back and forth
2. straight
3. round and round
4. up and down

E. 1. A. rolling
   B. turning
   C. spinning
2. bouncing
3. swinging
4. sliding

Try this!
Activity

8   Simple Machines

A. 1.

2.

3.

4.

5.

6.

B. 1. lever
2. wheel and axle
3. pulley
4. inclined plane
5. screw
6. wedge

C. 1.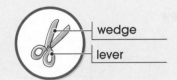
   wedge
   lever

2.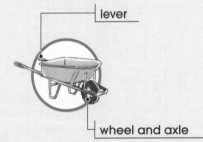
   lever
   wheel and axle

Try this!
a screw

9   Air in the Environment

A. 1. seeds   2. sailboat
   3. hot-air balloons 4. windmill
   5. plants

B. B ; E ; F
   A ; C ; D

C. 1. temperature
   2. thermometer
   3. degree Celsius
   4. A
   5. C
   6. B

D. 1. Burning trash, driving cars, and smoke from factories cause air pollution.
   2. Polluted air travels by wind.
   3. Polluted air mixes with water vapour to form acid rain.

Try this!
Activity

10   Water in the Environment

A. 1. A   2. E
   3. D   4. B
   5. C

B. 1. fog   2. snow
   3. hail   4. dew
   5. frost   6. rain

C. 1. well   2. river
   3. lake
   4. water treatment plant
   5. water supply system

D. C ; A ; D ; B
   (Individual suggestion)

Try this!
A

Final Review

A.

B. 1. A ; C ; D
    2. B
    3. A ; C
    4. A ; B ; E
    5. A ; D
    6. A ; C ; D

C. Colour the following.
    A. washing a car
    C. removing suds
    D. cleaning teeth
    F. pushing a kayak

D. 1. D
    2. F
    3. B ; A

E. 1. bouncing ; over
    2. turning ; on
    3. swinging ; under
    4. rolling ; behind

ISBN: 978-1-927042-84-7